Meet Ollie the dog, so friendly and keen, a golden retriever with a scarf bright green. Today he's off to the seaside to play, through busy beaches along the way. He loves to hide in places just right, so look very closely with all your might. On every page, wherever he goes, can you spot Ollie before the end shows?

Laughter and footsteps fill the seaside air, children climb and scramble everywhere. High on the platforms the fun's on the go, with splashes and cheers down below. Ollie looks up, tail wagging with glee, stretching up tall — can you spot where will he be?

Footsteps thump along the boardwalk by the sea, with buckets and boats and shells by the three. Sails flap and bob as they drift on the blue, while seagulls swoop down with a curious "coo!" Ollie loves rocking with waves up and down, floating and drifting away from the town. Look past the planks and out over the foam... Can you spot Ollie enjoying his boaty-day roam?

The seaside hums with music and cheer, footsteps and laughter are buzzing round here. Stalls line the boardwalk, waves shimmer and gleam, while boats gently sway like part of a dream. Ollie's feeling brave — and a teeny bit daring, testing his balance where people are staring. Look near the rail where the boardwalk bends... Can you spot Ollie wobbling — paws out, my friends!

Water on both sides shimmers and gleams, sand in the middle full of seaside dreams. Seagulls swoop low with calls in the air, while footsteps and laughter bustle everywhere. A long jetty stretches out into the blue, beach huts line up in bright colours too. Ollie loves hiding where shadows stay cool... Can you spot him tucked low, playing hide-and-seek rules?

The sea grows lively, splashing and wide, with sailboats dancing on the tide. A paddling pool sparkles with giggles and play, as little feet splash the day away. Far on the horizon, big ships glide slow, passing by where the deep waters flow. Ollie loves spots where the splashing is loud... Can you spot him nearby, not lost in the crowd?

Click-clack footsteps and laughter nearby, ice creams drip as runners pass by. Cameras flash and seagulls call, benches are busy — there's fun for all! Ollie weaves where the crowds go by, not too low... and not too high. Look where the boardwalk meets beachy cheer, a green scarf might be hiding right here!

The shore feels alive with splashes and cheer, waves tumble in as the boats draw near. Seagulls wheel high with calls so loud, dancing and dipping above the crowd. Mountains rise softly far off in the land, clouds drift lazily over sea and sand. Ollie loves places where everyone's free...Can you spot him among all the fun by the sea?

In the quiet bay, the water is calm, a peaceful place like a seaside psalm. Sailboats drift softly, side by side, as gentle breezes sweep the tide. Soft clouds wander across the blue, the world feels still and fresh and new. Ollie loves places peaceful and slow... Can you spot him resting where the breezes go?

By the edge of the sand, the lighthouse shines bright, watching the waves from morning to night. Its steady beam glides over the sea, guiding the boats as calm as can be. Nearby, little shops face the salty air, with chatter and laughter drifting everywhere. Ollie loves places where sea lights glow... Can you spot him close by, scarf green all aglow?

Rain patters softly on boardwalk and sand, in puddles it goes plop — how grand! Bright coloured markers peek out near the shore, paddling pools splash as the clouds start to pour. The lifeguard tower stands watch through the rain, while gum boots skip and splash again and again. Ollie loves puddles — he's having a ball... Can you spot him nearby, scarf green and all?

After the rain, when the sunshine is near, a rainbow appears, bright and clear. Ollie looks up with a wag and a grin, could he walk on those colours? Where would he begin? The rainbow dips low where the sand meets the sea, near towels and footprints and people with glee. Follow the colours right down to the ground. That's where Ollie and his green scarf might just be found.

As the sun sinks low and the sky turns gold, the beach feels cosy as the day grows old. People pause to watch as the colours gleam, with salty air and an evening dream. Where the light meets sand and shadows grow long, Ollie is hiding — just tagging along. Look near the glow where the warm hues blend, he's close to the day's bright, beautiful end.

The boardwalk stretches onward, all weathered and wide, past bustling little shops by the seaside. A lighthouse stands tall as the day drifts away, guiding the boats as they bob and they sway. Ollie's not far — he's still out having fun, after splashing and searching and chasing the sun. Look where the walkway meets lights warm and bright... Can you find Ollie one more time before saying goodnight?

Did you spot Ollie every time?

Through waves and sand and seaside rhyme? If you found him hiding on each page, well done — you're a super spotter for your age!

But Ollie's adventures don't end here, you see... he shares stories with a ginger cat named Ellie. Together they explore, help, learn, and play, in other adventures just a page away.

This story was created by Marina Swan, who loves bringing gentle adventures to life one by one. Inspired by nature, kindness, and curiosity too, she hopes The Adventures of Ellie and Ollie bring smiles to you.

Other books in this series

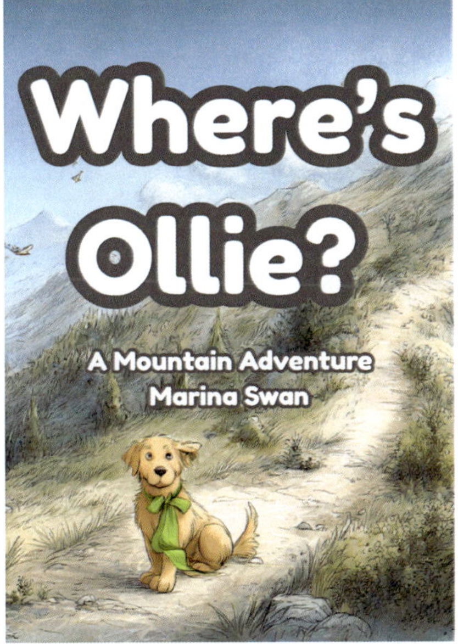

* 9 7 8 1 9 2 3 7 5 0 0 5 0 *